This is Frank Lloyd Wright

Published in 2016 by
Laurence King Publishing
361–373 City Road
London EC1V 1LR
United Kingdom
T +44 20 7841 6900
F +44 20 7841 6910
enquiries@laurenceking.com
www.laurenceking.com

ISBN: 978 1 78067 8566

Series editor: Catherine Ingram

Printed in China

This is
Frank Lloyd
Wright

IAN VOLNER

Illustrations by MICHAEL KIRKHAM

LAURENCE KING PUBLISHING

Frank Lloyd Wright was, during his eventful life, called "husband," "adulterer," "progressive," "reactionary," "idealist," "crook," "crackpot," "genius". And, incredibly, at one time or another, he really was all of these: his life was marked by dramatic shifts and reversals of fortune, and these changes were all the more striking as so many of them seemed to result from Wright's dogged pursuit of a single idea—a particular image of himself and of the world that he wanted to live in.

What was that image, and who exactly was Wright? Answers to these questions were elusive even at the time, and have since been further clouded by the perceptions of both critics and admirers alike. A prodigious teacher, Wright left an indelible, positive, mark on many of the students who came in and out of his studio—and alienated scores of others who called him a bully and a demagogue. The Wrightian cult of personality extended to his clients, typically wealthy sophisticates who came to him looking for nothing less than a work of art they could live in—and who came away, at least half the time, wondering where their money had gone. Even Wright's contributions to design are a matter of contention: much of his thinking about cities, buildings, and the designer's place in society have fallen out of favor. And yet his buildings—over 400 of them—are still so loved and his name is still so familiar to millions who might not be able to identify a single other architect. Who is this man that so many of us think we know? What did he do to make himself so well known, and yet so hard to know? Who is Frank Lloyd Wright?

The Wrights and the Lloyd Joneses

Wright was born on June 8, 1867 in Richland Center, Wisconsin. But the story—and the mythology—of Wright begins in Wales in the nineteenth century. Or that, at least, is what Wright himself liked to assert: his maternal grandfather, Richard Jones, was a good place to start for anyone keen to build a mythology of himself. Wright always regarded his immigrant forebear as a model, a daring religious nonconformist who left the Welsh countryside to become a pioneer in the American West with his wife, Mary Lloyd, and their seven children in tow. The origins of Wright's father, by contrast, were perhaps a little too small for Wright's outsized tastes: William Wright was a New Englander, a sometime clergyman and musician who never quite lived up to his own romantic ambitions—still less those of his imperious wife, Anna Lloyd Jones, and of her sprawling, prosperous clan. The Lloyd Joneses were key in the spread of Unitarianism in the US, in particular Wright's minister uncle, Jenkin Lloyd Jones. Wright's father began life as a Baptist, and preached as one during a brief stint in Massachusetts, but he, too, later became a Unitarian.

```
The landscape made the
greatest impression on
the young Wright. It became
fused with his family's faith
and with Transcendentalist
philosophy to make him a
lifelong adherent of a
kind of natural religion
```

```
"I believe in God,
 only I spell it 'Nature'."

Frank Lloyd Wright
```

The Valley

The setting for the Wright/Lloyd Joneses family drama, and for Wright's earliest memories, was the lush farm country around Spring Green in western Wisconsin. Here, Richard Jones had settled in the 1840s; here William and Anna met and were married in 1866, producing a son, Frank Lincoln Wright, followed by two girls. And, with the exception of a brief spell back East when William Wright (unhappily) led a congregation in Massachusetts, this is where the future architect spent all of his formative years, in the constant company of the assorted aunts, uncles, and cousins who lived nearby. The Valley, as the Lloyd Joneses called their little sliver of Wisconsin, wasn't just a place in which to grow up: it was a hothouse for the ideas that would be most influential to Wright, where the Lloyd Joneses' liberal Unitarian religion and the free-thinking philosophies of Ralph Waldo Emerson and Henry David Thoreau were as much a part of the landscape as the rivers, trees, and rolling hills.

The close-knit family
atmosphere of The Valley
included group outings,
group performances, and
group picnics. It instilled
a sense of belonging in the
children who grew up there.

Froebel

Every good mythology should start with a prophecy. And, sure
enough, Wright claimed that his mother was the prophet of his
life and that she had declared, even before he was born, that he
would build beautiful buildings. Clairvoyant or not, Anna had a
powerful interest in cultivating her son's intellect, a fixation on
little Frank's potential that steadily crowded out her affection
for her daughters and husband. Perhaps her most important
contribution to his education came while they were living in
Massachusetts, when she discovered a toy called Froebel Gifts:
before Lego and the Erector Set, German educator Friedrich
Froebel developed a simple series of colored, geometrical
wooden blocks. Their effect on little Frank would be profound.

In line with Froebel's
theory of "free play" as
the best stimulus to the
developing mind, the
blocks could be combined
and recombined ...

... to make different
assemblages and
different structures ...

... whose complex
forms, emerging from
simple volumes, ...

The dropout

The breaking point between Wright's mother and father came in 1884, when Wright was 16. The two separated and, while they did not formally divorce until the following year, this was the end of William's role in his son's life: Wright claimed he never saw his father again, and he effectively wrote the roving organist– preacher–intellectual out of his personal story. Yet, even as he drew closer to the Lloyd Jones fold and its happy, hearth-bound family life—even changing his middle name to Lloyd—the growing young man seemed as much his father's son as his mother's, in his inability to stick at anything. He was put to farm work by his uncle James, hated it, and ran away repeatedly. He dropped out of high school, and then out of the University of Wisconsin–Madison, where he had enrolled to study civil engineering. The only constant in his adolescent years was his fascination with architecture and his determination to pursue it. In order to do so he fled once again, at age 19, to Chicago, taking up work as a draftsman in the office of the architect Joseph Lyman Silsbee, whom he had assisted while at university. His tenure at this office (during which he actually quit, again, only to be rehired later) marked his entry into the design trade, a good portion of which was spent working on Lloyd Jones family projects in and around Spring Green. Now the chief breadwinner for his mother and sisters, Wright still put family very much at the center of his life, even as he made his lonely way in the great metropolis of the Midwest.

... look, in retrospect, like a glimpse of the architecture of the future.

Chicago circa 1887

Founded in 1833, Chicago grew rapidly. By mid-century, landscape architect Frederick Law Olmsted wrote that it was a city of flimsy wooden buildings, "over-weighted with gross and coarse mis-ornamentation." Between October 8 and 10, 1871, 2,000 acres of the city burned to the ground in the Great Chicago Fire. The "hot time in the old town," as the American ragtime song goes, turned out to be a great time for architects, who set about busily rebuilding the ruined city. By the time Wright arrived in 1887, Chicago was a city of over a million people and ground zero for a revitalized American architecture.

The new arrival didn't necessarily take to the town right away: it was a rough place, after all, where the Haymarket labor riot had broken out just a year before, and where Wright had to live on just $8 a week from Silsbee's office. But both the good and the bad in this new urban landscape would forever mark Wright's thinking.

Among the giants on the Chicago architecture scene was Henry Hobson Richardson, whose muscular, Romanesque-influenced

Rookery Building
Daniel Burnham
(1888)

Marshall Field's
H.H. Richardson
(1887)

buildings included the massive Marshall Field's Wholesale Store, opened in the Loop, the central business district, the very year that Wright arrived. Richardson was "just what America deserved," Wright said, "a powerful romantic eclectic."

Richardson's work stood in sharp contrast to that of another player in the city's reinvention. Daniel Burnham was the dean of Chicago architecture—"Uncle Dan," as his colleagues and clients called him. His own designs (including the famous Monadnock Building) varied in style from high Classical to Egyptian to proto-modern simplicity. But it was his grandiose, classicized plan for the "White City," the fairgrounds for the city's Columbian Exposition in 1893, that turned out to be his most influential project.

The fashionable Beaux Arts style ushered in by the Exposition didn't resonate with the young architect fresh from the prairies. But the work of another designer did: Louis Sullivan's buildings were simply stated and their facades sparingly and originally decorated in their creator's inventive, floral ornamented style. They seized Wright's imagination instantly.

Auditorium Building
Louis Sullivan
(1889)

The Master

"A small man immaculately dressed in brown. His outstanding feature his amazing big brown eyes. Took me in at a glance. Everything I felt, even to my utmost secret thoughts." Such was Wright's first impression of the man he would call afterwards, even into his old age, "Lieber Meister"(Dear Master). Louis Sullivan was the architect who coined the phrase "form follows function," the first architect to view the potential of the skyscraper as the essential building type for a new architecture and a new way of living in America. His essay "The Tall Office Building Artistically Considered" set out a clear, rational formula for high-rise design, dividing skyscrapers into three parts to reflect the different functional uses of the lowermost, middle, and upper stories. He also had an eye for talent and, recognizing Wright's at once, he swiftly poached the draftsman from Silsbee for his firm Adler & Sullivan.

Sullivan was an intimidating figure in the studio, and when Wright first joined as a draftsman he was in awe of the great man's genius and authority. As time went on, it was Sullivan who came to respect Wright—and, even years later, after the fortunes of both men had changed dramatically and not a little bad blood had come between them, it was Wright who Sullivan wanted at his bedside as he succumbed to years of alcoholism. "Don't leave me, Frank," he begged him; and in a way, Wright never did, remaining a devoted follower of his Lieber Meister.

Sullivan's Guaranty Building
Buffalo, New York, 1895–1896

First houses

Wright's early work for Sullivan mostly involved elaborating on the latter's design concepts. Sullivan's office was mostly devoted to large-scale commercial work, but when a favored (and sufficiently wealthy) client requested a house, the firm obliged—and Wright quickly rose to head up their residential practice.

The James A. Charnley House in Chicago was one early commission on which Wright worked. Modest and mostly plain-fronted, it was rich with interior ornament in the classic Sullivan-esque mode, and is still open today as a museum

The rising young draftsman also lent a hand to Sullivan's own vacation home in Ocean Springs, Mississippi. Wright sometimes claimed that the designs for this and other early houses had been more his than Sullivan's; sadly, would-be connoisseurs can no longer judge the bungalow for themselves, since it was destroyed by Hurricane Katrina in 2005.

James A. Charnley House
**Louis Sullivan and
Frank Lloyd Wright, 1892**
Chicago, Illinois

Mr and Mrs Wright

Wright had long claimed that women "terrified him," and his brief experience with them had comprised only a couple of abortive correspondences and a student mixer during his stint at the University of Wisconsin–Madison. This could only have been to his mother's liking: still keeping a watchful eye on her boy, Anna Wright's domineering character was doubtless one source of Wright's wariness of the opposite sex. But when he met 16-year-old Catherine (or Kitty) Lee Tobin, the architect cast off his erstwhile reticence. The two were married scarcely a year later and started a family almost immediately, overcoming every obstacle thrown in their path by the wealthier and better socially placed Tobins—to say nothing of the imperious Anna.

Much of Frank Lloyd Wright's early social life in Chicago revolved around his uncle Jenkin's All Souls Unitarian Church, where Kitty was also a member. Wright had spotted her there in the past but they didn't meet until some time later during a church-sponsored costume party—themed after Victor Hugo's novel *Les Misérables*—when the two physically collided on the dance floor. Their friendship progressed rapidly thereafter and, just weeks after her eighteenth birthday, they were wed. Anna Wright reportedly fainted during the ceremony.

Perhaps more revealing of Kitty's character than anything she said herself was what was said of her, years later, by one of her nieces. Aunt Kitty, she recalled, made her think of an old phrase: "Often in error but seldom in doubt."

Falling out

From the start, the lifestyle that Wright insisted upon for himself and his new family far outstripped his salary at Adler & Sullivan. Debts—for groceries, clothes, automobiles—mounted quickly. To keep up, Wright began taking on independent commissions, in express violation of his contract. These "bootleg" projects, which included the Walter Gale and Robert Parker houses, bore the hallmarks of Wright's Sullivan-influenced style, and when the elder architect caught wise in 1893 he was outraged. Wright insisted he had not broken faith with his Lieber Meister, but Sullivan swiftly fired him. The rupture between Sullivan and his prize pupil lasted 12 years.

The Steinway years

After setting up his own shop in Chicago's Sullivan-designed Schiller Building, Wright moved to a more capacious loft space in the nearby Steinway Hall. This was where he did his first independent work, and where he and a group of likeminded designers gave birth to a new style of architecture that became known as the Prairie School.

The first inhabitant of the eleventh floor space had been Dwight Perkins, a mild-mannered, MIT-educated Tennessean. He became best known through his designs for schools, building more than 40—all in the simple, geometrical mode of the Prairie School—for the Chicago Board of Education.

Robert C. Spencer, Jr., was a longtime acquaintance of Wright's, and it was he who brought Wright into the Steinway space. He also became a major proponent of Wright's work, penning major articles and essays describing his colleague's houses and advocating for the new style.

Then there was Myron Hunt, who Wright described as his "most enthusiastic advocate." The architect joined the fold at Steinway Hall after three years in Europe, but the tour abroad didn't deter him from pursuing projects in the distinctly American, non-Beaux Arts mode that Wright favored.

Among the first licensed female architects in the US, Marion Mahony demonstrated an instinctive feel for the long, simple lines of the Prairie Style, both in her own work and in her collaborations with Wright. Beginning her career alongside her cousin Dwight Perkins, she later became Wright's first official employee, and her watercolor renderings were key to winning over clients and bringing his work to a broader audience.

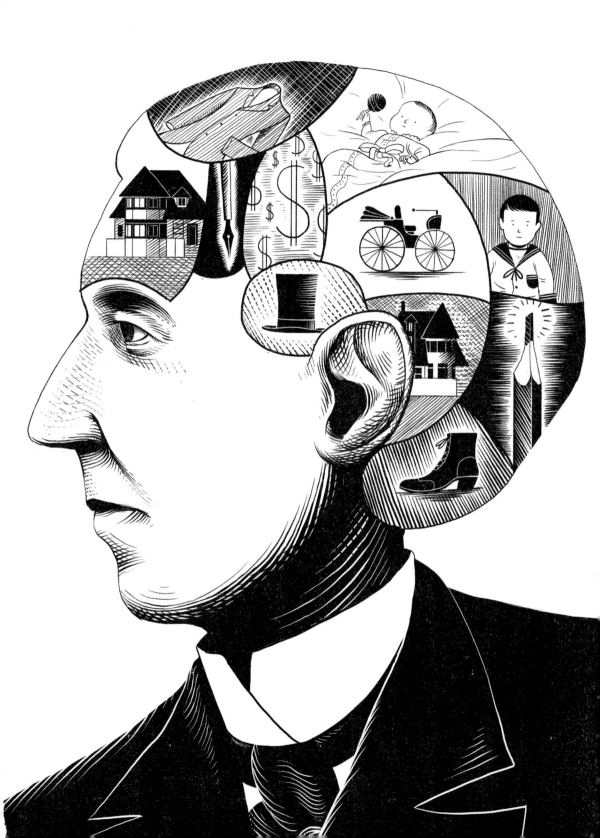

The Prairie School: neither school nor prairie?

It is easy enough to identify: big, overhanging eaves; sheltered entryways; capacious concrete planters; long bands of windows. The name seems explanation enough—a type of house native to and tailored for the wide, flat expanses of the American interior. But the Prairie School is not as simple or homogenous a movement as it's often thought to be. First there is the question of authorship: Wright is typically viewed, and viewed himself, as the father of the style. But the environment at Steinway Hall was a real cooperative workshop, and the evolution of Wright's houses accelerated at an incredible pace as soon as he came into contact with his fellow travelers. In addition, other architects unaffiliated with the school, such as Greene and Greene in California, were working along similar lines elsewhere, drawing on the same unacknowledged (by Wright, at least) sources as the Prairie designers—in particular the British-led Arts and Crafts movement, as well as the Shingle Style popular in the eastern US since the 1870s. Most of the Prairie School members weren't even from the prairie, and their work went in very different directions in their later careers, from high Art Deco to Spanish Colonial. If it *was* really "prairie," it was so almost by an accident of geography; and if it was a "school," then it was one in which Wright was not the principal, as he often proclaimed, but perhaps only its most illustrious graduate.

William Winslow House
Frank Lloyd Wright, 1893
River Forest, Illinois

Success comes to Frank

But what a graduate. In 1894, "Uncle Dan" Burnham, impressed by his work, tried to lure Wright to Europe with the promise of a fully paid spot at the École des Beaux-Arts in Paris. By the late 1890s, Wright found himself one of the most sought-after and highly paid domestic architects in the US. Wealthy professionals and industrialists in Chicago, upstate New York, and across the Midwest clamored for his Prairie designs; his writing for the *Ladies' Home Journal* made him a national tastemaker; and still he seemed to buzz with creative energy, his designs for houses moving from inspiration to inspiration.

Ward Willits House
Frank Lloyd Wright, 1901
Highland Park, Illinois

A home of their own

The Oak Park house at the corner of Forest and Chicago avenues that Wright shared with Kitty and their growing brood (five children within the first nine years of marriage) was acquired thanks to a $5,000 loan from Sullivan in 1889. Never content to leave well enough alone, Wright instantly set about modifying the original compound. By the time he moved his offices into the adjoining studio space he erected in 1898, he had made the structure into a version of his ideal home environment.

In the studio, the lofted ceiling, ringed with an internal balcony held aloft by chains, like a bridge, was flooded with light from above.

Here, in the studio, a besmocked Wright and his team could labor in peace and receive clients in style.

Wright's first employee was Marion Mahony, an important contributor to the Prairie School.

The second-floor playroom had a skylit barrel ceiling and lofted gallery where the children could present amateur theatricals, accompanied by the piano tucked discreetly under the staircase. Here, Kitty and the children were never too far from the busy paterfamilias next door.

The elevation exemplifies an early Wright-style, not the low Prairie roofline, but a pitched gable. More typical of the emerging Prairie School, however, is the extensive porch that wraps around the building.

Over time, the interior arrangement became more complex, culminating in the addition of the octagonal library and workshop flanking the reception area.

The mountebank of Oak Park

Success suited Wright. Kitty wore elaborate dresses, designed for her by her husband; the family tooled around town in a new Stoddard-Dayton roadster, one of the first automobiles in Oak Park; Christmases at the Wright house were grand affairs; and always, year round, they entertained—"clambakes, tea parties in his studio, cotillions in the large drafting room; gay affairs about the blazing logs that snapped and crackled in the big fireplace," as his son John would recall. The boy would also note his father's singular solicitousness with his female acquaintances: "The younger ones … seemed to swoon whenever he touched them."

Victorian homes, Victorian notions

High principles and conservative tastes were the norm during this period in the US, and that extended to Oak Park. Wright saw a vivid and disconcerting parallel between the hypocrisy of these moralistic Midwesterners and the flimsy facades of their houses: "The wood butchery" with which his competitors ornamented their creations, Wright said, was indicative of their "fashionable and unholy but entirely moral" architecture. Ridding his interiors of Victorian bric-a-brac, simplifying his exterior elevation, Wright was heralding a new form of domestic life. His freewheeling private life was going against the grain as well, attracting almost as much attention from his conventional, conformist neighbors.

"The Art and Craft of the Machine"

In breaking with the prevailing Beaux Arts style espoused by "Uncle Dan" Burnham and others, Wright wasn't just challenging stylistic orthodoxy. He was, in a real sense, questioning the whole political, economic, and cultural status quo of his time. "Upon this faith in Art as the organic heart … of the scientific frame of things, I base a belief that we must look to the artist brain, of all brains, to grasp the significance to society of this thing we call the Machine," he wrote in his pioneering 1901 essay, "The Art and Craft of the Machine": in this utopian vision, an inspired creative class would fuse together technology and nature to bring about a harmonious new social order. It was a vision that found expression in projects such as the Larkin Administration Building, an office tower in Buffalo, New York, organized around an airy, light-filled atrium, with every piece of furniture purpose-built by Wright's office. It was visible, too, in such small details as the original ornamental details applied to his houses. "A new definition and new direction must be given the art activity of the future," he wrote. Time would bear out just how radical his new art was to be.

Larkin Administration Building
Frank Lloyd Wright, 1904–1906
Buffalo, New York

Dark and dim when first entered, the interior opened up dramatically once the visitor reached the light-charged central court, with its glazed ceiling and open gallery floors.

And then there was Mamah ...

It was not only in the realm of work that Wright sought a new direction. But what was it that made him turn the cold shoulder to his wife of nearly two decades? Perhaps he had simply become restless in the role of head of the family; perhaps tribulations in his extended family (his uncle James died suddenly in an accident in 1907) left him seeking additional solace; or, perhaps, he was reenacting his own father's abandonment ... Still, how could the man who extolled home and hearth in his writings and designs give up on the idyll of family life? Much as he loved them, Wright was in so many ways too much the rebellious child himself to feel like a father to anyone. He always referred to the six children he had with Kitty as "her children." And then there was Martha Cheney (known as Mamah), the new object of his affections: like him, she was a perpetual outsider, someone who felt herself at odds with her time and place.

Kitty Wright met the married Mamah at Oak Park's popular Nineteenth Century Women's Club. The Cheneys and the Wrights became fast friends and, in 1903, Wright finished work on a new house for the couple. Wright and Mamah found they shared a special connection; her intelligence and progressive thinking seeming to echo Wright's own. With her, Wright was able to imagine he had found a higher ideal of companionship, a partnership that defied the very social conventions he was overturning with his new buildings.

Ornament

When Wright conceived the decorative programs of his buildings—colorful bursts of glass, carved concrete, sculpted stone—it was not simply to relieve the facade, but to express the spirit of the place and time.

Feminist, intellectual, renegade

Unusually for a woman of her time, Mamah had pursued not just
an undergraduate degree but a master's as well, and she spoke
German, French, Italian, and Spanish, and was also literate in
Greek and Latin. In another time or place, she would certainly
have been a professional woman in her own right, an academic or
a writer; had she not come from a staid, middle-class background
(her father was a railroad superintendent), she might have been
a radical suffragist, smashing shop windows and agitating for the
vote. As it was, she was only a rather frustrated housewife, full
of inchoate yearnings that she had little time or opportunity to
pursue. The flamboyant, artistic Wright, similarly dissatisfied in
married life, awakened something within her.

The Stoddard-Dayton was nicknamed the Yellow Devil, and on
many bright mornings Wright might be seen riding in it beside
the woman whom, years later, his children would still recall as
his "fair companion"—Mamah Cheney, the wife of his client, the
affable and much-admired Edwin Cheney.

Rollin Furbeck House
(1897)

Arthur Heurtley House
(1902)

Peter A. Beachy House
(1906)

Mamah and Wright spent hours chatting, their conversations beginning with the house Wright was designing for her and her husband but soon veering towards deeper, more intimate matters. Kitty Wright began to notice something awry in her relationship with her husband as early as 1905—a growing distance between the two—and she soon began to resent how attached Wright had become to her sometime friend.

Neither did Wright's friends and neighbors fail to notice how close the two had become, and the illicit couple became the talk of Oak Park, or "Saints' Rest" as the town was often called, a place with more churches than bars. Wright was risking everything, not least the censure of the tight-knit community that had helped make his reputation.

Laura Gale House
(1909)

Stalling

Not just in his private life, but in his professional life, by the end of the decade Wright began to feel that he had lost his sense of purpose. "Weary, I was losing grip on my work, and even interest in it," he later recalled; the single-family homes that had sustained him for so many years no longer held his attention, and he had carried the Prairie Style as far as he could. More frustratingly still, the major commercial and institutional projects that Wright longed for didn't seem to be coming, and even a major residential commission, for the home of the wealthy Rockefeller McCormick family, slipped away from him. Wright was at an impasse.

Looking for something new

In his quest for a way forward, Wright began to look further afield. As early as 1893, he had seen and been much impressed by the Japanese temple that was featured at the Columbian Exposition. Shortly thereafter, the architect began to collect Japanese woodblock prints and, in 1905, he and Kitty traveled together for the first time to Japan. Together with the Willitses, the clients for whom Wright had designed one of his most iconic Prairie houses, the Wrights explored the country's landscape, architecture, and culture. (Wright embraced the local customs with particular gusto: he took to wearing a traditional robe during his stay, but his client's wife cut their trip short early after Wright took Ward Willits to a traditional Japanese bath house with an all-woman staff.) Along the way, Wright built up his collection of Japanese art and artifacts, primarily prints, screens, and porcelain.

Wright was never shy about the influence of Japanese art and design on his own work, but it was never simply a recapitulation of Japanese style, as such. As he wrote to a friend in 1910, he "digested" it, transforming the openness and simplicity of Japan's building culture into something suited to the American landscape. In some respects, however, Wright was content to play copycat. His signature was a prime example: in around 1904, he abruptly switched from the Celtic cross that had long marked his work papers and letters to a cartouche (his initials contained within a light umber frame). The symbol is plainly meant to recall the ideograms of East Asian calligraphy.

Unity and Robie

Even as he tired of Chicago, becoming more and more disenchanted with his life and his practice there, Wright still managed to turn out two masterpieces—the capstones to the first phase of his career.

The Unity Temple, begun in 1905 and completed three years later, marked a return to Wright's roots, in a sense, the Universalist rite being not too unlike the Unitarian faith of Wright's upbringing. The forward-thinking congregation was a good fit for Wright's innovative design solution: an all-reinforced concrete structure, among the first of its kind in the US.

It is, at first sight, Wright's most daunting building, a gray bunker whose entrance, on a traffic-filled street, rears up from the sidewalk on a monumental porch. But, once inside, the interior lives up to its name: it is a fully unified composition, with indirect light filtering in through stained-glass windows above, imparting what the critic Vincent Scully once called the building's "special singleness," its "unequaled continuity."

The apogee of the Prairie house was reached in the Robie House, built between 1908 and 1910: like Unity, it was structurally and materially innovative, with the client's relatively lavish budget helping to underwrite a steel frame that allowed the broad eaves to be drawn out to their fullest extent.

That horizontality is picked up again by the exterior pattern in Wright's favored Roman bricks, long and slender to accentuate the flat line of the house. Inside, as at Unity, there is an alternation between light and dark spaces, the nearly windowless foyer giving way to the light-filled living spaces above.

The ill-starred Robies would live in it for scarcely a year before falling into financial hardship and divorce. And their architect hadn't even been on hand to complete it ...

Unity Temple
Frank Lloyd Wright
1905–1908
Oak Park, Illinois

Robie House
Frank Lloyd Wright
1908–1910
University of Chicago,
Chicago, Illinois

Extra, extra!
Read all about it!

STRANGE INFATUATION

TWO ABANDONED HOMES!

STRANGE INFATUATION

Fly by Night JOURNEY THROUGH GERMANY!

TRAMPLED UPON AND SPURNED!

Flight

In the middle of 1909 Mamah had gone to Boulder, Colorado, and Wright to New York. A German publisher, Ernst Wasmuth, had offered to prepare a major volume of Wright's complete architectural opus if he would come to Germany and join in the effort. Wright used this as a pretext to extract a $10,000 loan from a client, a fellow Japanese-print collector. Holing up in the Plaza Hotel, New York, he waited while Mamah wrote her husband to come and pick up the children. She then set out for the East Coast herself. For several weeks the two lingered in Manhattan, preparing for what would be Wright's first-ever sojourn to Europe. Then they struck out together—to Berlin, first, where the newspapers caught up with them. Kitty was hurt but remained, astonishingly, committed to her husband; Anna, for once, took her daughter-in-law's part; Edwin Cheney almost immediately began divorce proceedings.

New home in the Old World

From Berlin the couple traveled south, setting up shop in a small villa called Fortuna in the town of Fiesole, just outside Florence. Mamah took up a teaching post at a school in Berlin, and the two spent much of the year splitting their time between Tuscany and Germany. Wright sent for his eldest child, Lloyd, to help him with the still-developing Wasmuth volume, and his son arrived to find his father happily installed in Italy, strolling around in the evenings with Mamah through the "opalescent, iridescent" landscape. They were, to all appearances, incredibly happy.

TWO ABANDON[ED] [H]OME[S]

WRIGHT HAS LOST ALL SENSE OF MORALITY!

Learning from Europe

After all his determined polemics about forging a new American
architecture free of European influences, Wright was swept
away by the beauty of the ancient city. He dipped into Vasari,
the great historian of Renaissance art, and into John Ruskin, the
English architecture theorist who had been a forefather to the Arts
and Crafts movement. He spent hours admiring the work of that
"wondrous brood of Florentines," the great Renaissance sculptors
and painters whose work adorned the churches and palazzos of
the town. Even his modest *villino*, the Fortuna, managed to charm
hyper-critical Wright, its "small solid door framed in the solid
white blank wall" bearing all the promise of domestic sanctuary.
Even running away from home, he was still a homebody at heart.

No honor in his own country

But Wright's time abroad was to prove more than just a
romantic idyll. The Wasmuth portfolio, which the publishing
house issued in 1910, burst like a thunderclap on the European
scene, exerting an outsized influence on a whole generation
of architects. Under the German title *Ausgeführte Bauten und
Entwürfe von Frank Lloyd Wright*, the folio, in two separate
volumes, which included 100 lithographs chronicling the bulk
of his architectural output to date, found its way into the hands of
key design thinkers of the emerging Modernist movement. His
reputation on "the Continent" was being made—even as it was
being ripped apart back home ...

Upstarts

The Berlin office of architect Peter Behrens was something of
a clearing house for young architects in the second decade
of the twentieth century, and Behrens himself owned a copy
of the Wasmuth portfolio. Among his pupils was a Swiss-born
architect named Charles-Édouard Jeanneret-Gris—soon to
be known to the world as Le Corbusier. Another of Behrens's
younger associates was fellow German Ludwig Mies van der
Rohe, whose early villas—not yet reduced to the pure planar
forms of his later work—already strived toward something
like the smooth spatial flow of Wright's houses, and only his
conservative clients kept him from applying flat roofs to several
of them as Wright had done at Robie.

Walter Gropius rounded out Behrens's team of prodigies and
he, too, found Wright's work a revelation—calling him the only
significant architect whose "artistic evolution" matched the
"technical organization" he so admired in American buildings.

Gropius

Mies van
der Rohe

Le Corbusier

Kitty kept a "day book" chronicling life in the Wright house without Wright, ever expectant of his return.

TRUTH IS LIFE.

GOOD FRIEND, AROUND THESE
HEARTH-STONES SPEAK NO EVIL
WORD OF ANY CREATURE···

That vampire woman!

Kitty's and Wright's son David was shocked at the bills his father left behind. $900 for groceries alone!

Frank and Mamah

Of all the parties to the tangled Wright-Cheney affair, there is one portion we know least about: the actual character of the relationship between Wright and Mamah Borthwick (who reverted to her maiden name after Edwin granted her a divorce). Few letters between them survive; and Wright himself, in his own autobiography, is curiously silent about the woman he refers to only as "her who, by force of rebellion as by way of love was then implicated with me." With so much between them— Mamah's incipient feminism, Wright's mercurial romanticism, children left behind, futures uncertain—it could not always have been easy for them in Europe. Wright drafted a home and studio for them in Fiesole, but the plan was soon abandoned and, after so many days "walking hand in hand miles through the hot sun" of Italy, they returned to the US.

Going home

Wright considered, in a rather self-exculpatory way, that in the year he spent apart from Kitty and the children he was living out the dream of self-realization and daring independence necessary for a "Great Artist." The folks back home certainly obliged, making him feel like a pariah when he returned: friends turned their backs on him, the papers bayed for his blood. Only Kitty seemed relieved to have him back—though she could hardly have known for how long.

It would appear that the demands of a domestic life with Kitty and "her children," surrounded by his erstwhile friends, and with bills pouring in, held no greater allure for Wright now than it had before he went away. Scarcely back in the family fold, Wright began laying plans to rent out his former Oak Park studio, to provide an income for his wife and children. He, along with Mamah, his "faithful companion" and his mother Anna (who had once again taken his part against Kitty's), would remove to an altogether different, if no less familiar, locale.

Taliesin

In Welsh Taliesin means "Shining Brow," from the name of a
legendary medieval bard in the homeland of Wright's forebears.
To escape the attention of newspapermen, and the disapproving
glares of his Chicago neighbors, Wright escaped back into
history, his own family's history—returning to Spring Green and
to the district near the Lloyd Joneses' beloved Valley, where he
would build his ideal home for a renewed ideal of family life.

A house entirely of its element, it was made from yellow
limestone quarried locally and dragged to the site by his farmer
neighbors; but it was also reminiscent—with its commanding
views of the landscape and its situation not *on top* of but *in* the
hillside—of the *palazzi* Wright and Mamah had seen while
abroad. Wright created a palace of nature, a fortress where he
could, as he put it, "get my back against the wall and fight for
what I saw I had to fight."

He wasn't fighting alone. The money to buy the plot was Anna's,
and a whole cluster of colorful local craftsman pitched in to build
the house, most of them immigrant laborers who, Wright said,
"were soon as interested as sculptors fashioning a statue," lending
their own artistic sensibility to the laying of the heavy masonry
chimneys and the stone walkways that wound through the site.

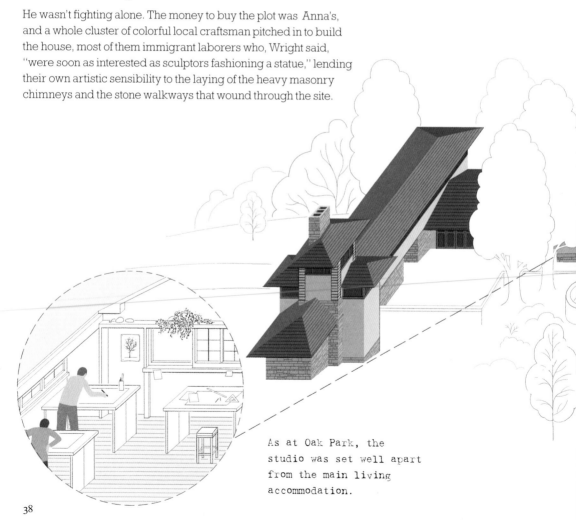

As at Oak Park, the
studio was set well apart
from the main living
accommodation.

38

Sheltered within, there was a modest courtyard around a Japanese-inspired "tea circle," a limestone perch surrounding a small pool. This, in turn, was encircled by the gracious (but at 12,000 square feet—just over 1,100 square meters—by no means massive) structure of the house itself, the various volumes containing the connected studio and living spaces arrayed around the courtyard in a J-like configuration.

The rooms were walled in plaster that Wright and his workers mixed with sand from nearby riverbeds, and all through the day the interiors would gleam with the rays of the sun, the windows placed so that every room had natural light. In winter, one would look outside and see icicles dangling from the eaves—Wright deliberately omitted gutters to encourage their growth.

And, everywhere, Wright ordered the planting of lush vegetation, "strawberry beds, white, scarlet, and green … abundant asparagus … green and yellow grapes … "

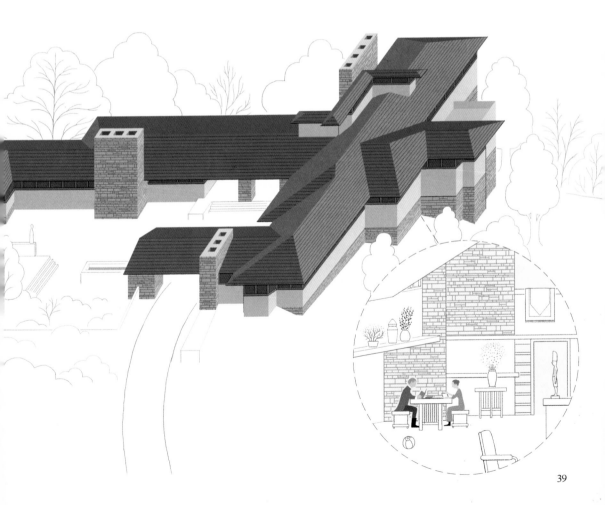

Struggling

The need to resume his life and his work was part of what had impelled the return to the US. But the return to normalcy did not come. Having escaped Oak Park and Kitty a second time, the Chicago newspapers were not long in finding him and Taliesin was soon splashed across front pages nationwide. The number of projects he executed in the following decade was scarcely half the number he had completed in the decade prior. Among the few bright spots during what are often referred to as Wright's "lost years" was a commission for Midway Gardens, a beer garden, dance hall and park complex in Chicago. Wright commuted back and forth from Taliesin to oversee its design and rapid construction in 1914.

Life at Taliesin

Taliesin, Wright said, was to be many things: "an architect's workshop," "a dwelling," "a farm cottage," "a recreation ground for my children and their children." Inside this mini-community, Mamah's son and daughter, Wright's studio hands, and many others besides would gather for entertainments, meals, work, and play. Defying the opprobrium of their rural neighbors, the Taliesin crew made up a cheery world of their own.

Whenever Wright was absent working on the Midway project, Mamah "took charge of the drafting room," reported Wright's son John, "and carried on her … translations and other writings." In the summer Mamah's children visited. John, 12, and Martha, eight, were not known to have been particularly fond of the house though they could have had no premonition of what was to happen there.

Death at Taliesin

Six workmen was about the usual complement of Wright's associates on hand at Taliesin. By the summer of 1914, they included 35-year-old carpenter, Billy Weston, who had helped build much of the house, as well as his 13-year-old son Ernest.

The communal character of life at Taliesin did have limits, and the whole house was arranged to make a certain distinction between those who lived there and those who came there to work. Separate dining rooms were provided for each. Both, however, were served by the same kitchen and wait staff. That summer, the staff included Barbadian-born Julian Carlton, aged 30, and his wife Gertrude.

On Saturday, August 15, 1914, Carlton, after serving lunch to Mamah and the children, attacked them with a shingle axe. He then took a can of gasoline he had removed from the garage and set fire to the living quarters of Taliesin. At some point, he moved over to the where the workmen were having lunch, locked the door to their dining room, started a blaze at the door, and then waited outside ready to attack any of the six men inside trying to escape.

Awful news

That same day: "Mr Wright, you're wanted on the telephone …" Wright and his son John were in the middle of lunch in the grounds of the Midway Gardens in Chicago when the call arrived. He stepped out to take it and when he returned, he looked stricken. A tense silence followed. "What's happened, Dad?" asked John. The call had been from Wright's friend in Madison, Frank Roth, informing him about the fire at Taliesin. Wright and John dashed to Union Station, picking up their lawyer along the way, and together they took the only train available to southern Wisconsin, a slow local—in a compartment they shared, incredibly, with none other than Edwin Cheney, whom they encountered standing in the sweltering heat on the platform.

The train was met by a mob when it reached Madison. But Wright would not leave his compartment, and would not speak to the press, until he and his party finally arrived in Spring Green, shortly after ten o'clock at night.

"A long distance call from Spring Green.
'TALIESIN DESTROYED BY FIRE.'
But no word came of the ghastly tragedy itself. I learned of that little by little on my way home on the train that evening. The newspaper headlines glared with it."

John Lloyd Wright

Shock and aftermath

In all, seven people died, not counting Carlton himself, who hid in the basement of Taliesin as the house burned and then consumed acid when some of the neighbors, who had raced to the fire, discovered him many hours later next to the asbestos-lined furnace. It took him over a month to die and, during that interval, he offered little explanation for his actions. The only motive that has ever been convincingly imputed to this man, previously known as quietly reliable, if somewhat withdrawn, is that he suffered a psychotic break, precipitated in part by racial remarks made by at least one of his Taliesin workmates. All that is certain is what he did. Billy Weston, who grappled with Carlton and then dashed to a nearby farmer for help, lived to tell the tale and helped save the studio portion of the house. But his young son perished, along with three of their fellow workmen, Mamah Borthwick, and her two children, John and Martha Cheney.

"Taliesin Burning
to the Ground!

SEVEN SLAIN!"

Starting over

"I cut her garden down and with the flowers filled a strong, plain box of fresh, white pine to overflowing … We made the whole a mass of flowers. It helped a little." Wright buried Mamah in the churchyard at Unity Chapel, the family church he had helped design with Silsbee. The weeks and months that followed were hard on him. He developed boils on his back and neck. He may have courted suicide, standing on the banks of a nearby river when it flooded. He was swept away but he survived, and he vowed to rebuild. An appreciative note from Wright to his Spring Green neighbors appeared in the local paper only five days after the fire. Speaking of Taliesin, he closed on a defiant note: "My home will still be there."

Within less than a year of the tragedy, Wright had substantially rebuilt his Wisconsin refuge. Taliesin II was practically indistinguishable from its predecessor, only slightly larger, with an additional wing and connecting breezeway.

Wright would live and work there for another ten years. And then, one spring night in 1925, he was finishing dinner when, walking into the courtyard, he saw smoke pouring out of his bedroom window. Another fire—this time started by faulty telephone wiring—burned down the living quarters of Taliesin II in fairly short order, though it spared Wright's atelier.

And, yet again, Wright set to work. The third and final iteration of Taliesin was completed—thanks to a generous subscription taken up by Wright's friends and associates—in 1926, and on a bigger scale even than before, some 37,000 square feet (as compared to 12,000 for Taliesin I—or 3,400 square meters compared to 1,100).

Nor was this the end of Wright's combustion-born woes. In 1932, a small blaze broke out in Taliesin's apprentice quarters. In the years that followed, a brush fire Wright had started burned down part of the nearby Hillside School—the building he had designed for his maiden aunts—and a gasoline drum exploded in the Taliesin garage, burning it to the ground. Apprentices reported seeing him, late in life, walking up and down muttering to himself: "All my life I have been plagued by fire."

Taliesin
Frank Lloyd Wright, 1914
(rebuilt 1915, 1926)
Iowa County, Wisconsin

Work and the search for work

Sympathy, in certain quarters, for Wright's recent misfortunes did not unfortunately extend to granting him additional commissions for large-scale projects. World War I had broken out the very week before the first Taliesin disaster, and the ensuing economic uncertainty worsened the prospects for new work. Wright had to cast a wider net to find projects, looking beyond the Midwestern and East Coast businessmen who had long formed the bulk of his client base. And the projects he designed began to change, too— acquiring a tougher, heavier quality, and a still more complex spatial organization, that might be attributed to his own changed psyche following the events of 1914.

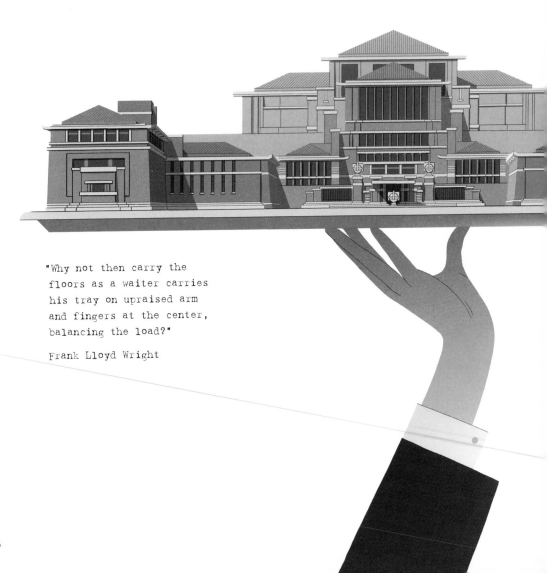

"Why not then carry the
floors as a waiter carries
his tray on upraised arm
and fingers at the center,
balancing the load?"

Frank Lloyd Wright

The Imperial Hotel

A team of Japanese hoteliers had combed the US looking for the best in American architecture, and they believed they'd found it in Wright's houses.

Two hundred and thirty rooms; a post office; stores and restaurants; the Peacock Room, seating a thousand diners; a theater below for a thousand more—The Imperial Hotel, Tokyo: this was a project that outstripped for sheer grandeur anything Wright had done before. The final price tag came in at over $4.5 million, more than $100 million in today's dollars.

Stylistically, the building was not necessarily Wright's most accomplished work, resembling—in its pitched roofs and abundant ornament—a faintly Asian-esque Prairie Style, with elements of Mayan design (a new preoccupation of Wright's) thrown in for good measure.

But, structurally, it was definitely innovative. Wright designed the building (or chain of buildings, articulated by separation joints) atop a deeply piled foundation, over which the light materials of the building would float as "a battleship floats on saltwater." This, he contended, would help the building escape damage during the frequent earthquakes that struck the Japanese capital.

Wright's hypothesis was put to the test twice, first in 1922 and then again, more seriously, a year later, when the city was struck by the Great Tokyo–Yokohama Earthquake of 1923. The 7.9-magnitude tremor killed over 100,000 people and destroyed upwards of a half a million homes, but the Imperial Hotel remained standing—"a monument of your genius," as one of its proprietors notified Wright in a cable shortly afterward.

Well, sort of. Both earthquakes did damage the hotel, the latter one quite extensively. Floors buckled, the central pavilion slumped. Though not many, there were buildings in Tokyo that fared better, and the hotel's relatively light damage was at least partially due to its being located at the periphery of the quake. But, naturally, Wright declined to mention either fact when he trumpeted the triumphant telegram to the Western press.

California

Wright received the good news about the Imperial while he was in Los Angeles, a city of which he'd became a regular habitué by the early 1920s. In retrospect, it seems only natural: the city's status as refuge for foreign émigrés, its bohemian film colony, and its overall reputation as the land of self-reinvention made LA a good fit for Wright's tastes and character.

"Any house should be beautiful in California," he wrote, "in the way that California herself is beautiful." First, in 1921, there was Hollyhock House, which was overseen largely by a new assistant of Wright's, a Viennese designer named Rudolph Schindler, who was among those young Europeans so enamored of Wright's work as seen in the Wasmuth portfolio.

Hollyhock demonstrated two of Wright's new preoccupations, which were to recur throughout his West Coast work: printed, pre-cast concrete-block construction and Meso-American design motifs.

These devices appeared again at La Miniatura in 1923 and Ennis House in 1924. The stacked blocks bore geometric patterns whose simplicity recalled the artwork of the Mayans and the Aztecs, but Wright's ambition for these blocks was more than for them to serve as a canvas for ornament: he believed the building system would make construction easier, and cheaper, than conventional techniques.

He was not, in the main, correct: Miniatura went 70 percent over its original $10,000 budget, and all the houses have suffered terribly from leaks ever since their completion.

They still look good on camera, though. Ennis House had a memorable turn decades later as the futuristic apartment house in sci-fi movie classic *Blade Runner.*

Hollyhock House
Frank Lloyd Wright
1919–1921
Los Angeles, California

Ennis House
Frank Lloyd Wright, 1924
Los Angeles, California

Furniture

For as long as he had been designing houses, Wright had been designing furniture with which to fill them. So complete was his conception of the harmonious environment that his clients often found there was no place to put such things of their own as they already had: living in a Frank Lloyd Wright house meant living inside a *Gesamtkunstwerk*—a complete work of art—committing fully to his values and vision.

The chairs often featured high backs and low seats in an effort to impart a feeling of empowerment to the sitter, a throne-like aspect that, unfortunately, is rarely comfortable, especially for taller people.

Other seating—banquettes and benches—was often built in, as were shelving, closets, and cabinets. Such storage options were all the more important given Wright's aversion to providing his houses with basements.

Lighting, too, was an essential part of Wright's fixture fixation, and it came in a beguiling variety of forms, from standing lamps to spectacular ceiling pendants to built-in stained-glass panels lit from behind.

And it wasn't just the usual interior decor that got the Wright treatment. He also placed his imprimatur on his buildings' gates, ventilation grates, powder-room vanities ... and even the things he didn't design himself, he specified to his tastes. His preoccupation with Pullman train cars found its way into the prefabricated tub-sink combination he installed in some of his bathrooms. The very dimensions of his interiors were scaled to suit not the client, but Wright himself: at 5 feet $8\frac{1}{2}$ inches, his (by today's standards) modest stature accounts for the snug feel of many of his projects.

By paying attention in his designs to every aspect of living, Wright was able to put into practice his dictum: "To thus make of a dwelling place a complete work of art ... this is the modern American opportunity."

To thus make of a dwelling place a complete work of art
THIS IS THE MODERN AMERICAN OPPORTUNITY

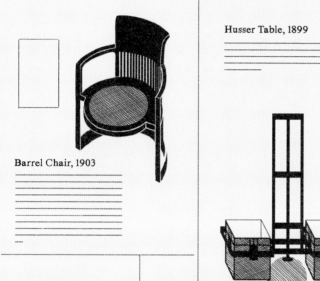

Barrel Chair, 1903

Husser Table, 1899

Unity Temple Light Fixture, 1908

Dana Sumac Vase, 1902

Robie 1 Chair, 1908

Taliesin 1 Lamp, 1923

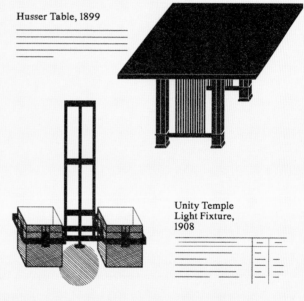

Catching up, falling behind

Wright's theory of what he had come to call "organic architecture"—the design of fully integrated environments, inspired by and in concert with the natural world—was a radical one when it first emerged after the turn of the century. But, by the mid-1920s, neither it nor its creator were any longer at the forefront of the profession. Developments in Europe, as well as Wright's altered standing on the domestic scene, put him out of sync with a rising avant-garde—a group of young designers, mostly European and many of them influenced by Wright himself, who were pursuing a new and different path.

"Men live in old houses and have not yet thought of building houses adapted to themselves." Only a decade out of Behrens's office, Le Corbusier hurled a rhetorical grenade at the architecture world with his book *Toward an Architecture*. In it, he spelled out how far design had fallen behind the times when it came to creating domestic environments appropriate to the age of the telephone, the automobile, and the airplane. "A house is a machine for living in," he wrote, and he took dead aim at the "cult of the home" so dear to Wright with his design of Villa Savoye in 1928.

Walter Gropius had come of age, too. Praising America as "the motherland of industry," he discarded Wright's organicism and instead married his unified design approach to the aesthetic of the factory and the grain elevator. The result was his Bauhaus school in Dessau, Germany: completed in 1926, the glass-enclosed complex was to be an incubator for a brace of radical artists and designers, turning out furniture, buildings, and more with the same focus on clarity, economy, and innovative materials and structure.

Drifting in and out of the Bauhausian fold was Mies van der Rohe, whose austere, reductive vision finally found a client ready to live with it in the Villa Tugendhat in Brno, then in Czechoslovakia. Ordered, restrained, almost neo-classical in its sense of proportion, Mies's emerging approach was perhaps the one most at odds with Wright's lush romanticism. It would also, in the years to come, be the approach that would serve the most direct challenge to Wright, and on his home turf.

Villa Savoye
Le Corbusier, 1928–1931
Poissy, France

The Bauhaus Building
Walter Gropius, 1925–1926
Dessau, Germany

Villa Tugendhat
Ludwig Mies van der Rohe, 1930
Brno, Czech Republic

Wright marries again …

On Christmas Day, 1914, Wright received a letter from an unknown woman. Ringing with high-flown phrases and slightly overwrought sentiment, it expressed sympathy for Wright's misfortunes and a desire to meet in person. The writer was Maude "Miriam" Noel and, for the next 13 years of Wright's life, she was a source of more crisis than comfort as she slid deeper and deeper into morphine addiction and mental illness.

From the moment she stepped into his Chicago office, Miriam made a singular impression. Tall, slender, extravagantly dressed, she was, like Wright, a self-dramatist of the first order, albeit in a far darker and (appropriately, given her southern background) distinctly gothic vein. They became romantically involved almost instantly, and Miriam moved into Taliesin shortly thereafter. Unlike the retiring Mamah, Miriam was outspoken in defense of her unconventional cohabitation with Wright, attracting still more media attention—as well as the attention of the authorities, who investigated them for violation of the arcane Mann Act, which forbade the transportation of women across state lines for "immoral purposes." (Formal charges were never brought.) Kitty finally granted Wright a divorce in 1922, and he and Miriam married when it became final the following year. However, as she was likely an undiagnosed schizophrenic, the relationship swung perilously from extreme to extreme, and they separated within a year. In the last of their melodramatic scenes, Miriam was banished from Taliesin in the middle of the night. Yet she continued to dog Wright for years, refusing to consent to a divorce until 1927.

Lord of my waking dreams!

And again …

While still legally married to Miriam, Wright was introduced
to Olgivanna Ivanovna Lazovich when they both attended a
performance by the Russian ballerina Tamara Karsavina in
Chicago. Olgivanna was 26, Wright was 57, and he was instantly
taken by the beautiful, elusive foreigner who was veiled in an air
of mystery. Olga, as she was known, was a prize pupil of Georges
Ivanovich Gurdjieff, a Russo-Armenian charismatic spiritualist
who had schooled her in the ways of his "sacred dance" during
her long expatriate years in Paris. Within a few months, Olga
followed Mamah and Miriam as the official woman of the
household at Taliesin.

Still scandalous

Olga was the last in the succession of wives and lovers that had
begun with Kitty Tobin some 40 years prior. But, finding her did
not mean that Wright had found peace and quiet at last. Their
relationship was stormy, their fights bitter, often punctuated
with walk-outs or the threat of walk-outs. Legal difficulties
dogged the couple at every turn: first Miriam threatened to sue
Wright, then she sued Olga; then Olga's ex-husband Vlademar

Finding oneself is the first
necessity. By proceeding from
within outward we find the
reality within. Only when we
have found it, will we be a
contributing power ...

Hinzenberg appeared on the scene and demanded custody of his daughter, Svetlana; next, Miriam followed through on her threat to sue Wright; and then she insisted that a warrant be issued for Wright's arrest for violation of the Mann Act. Wright and Olga were duly arrested in Minnesota, where they had gone into hiding, and were obliged to pay out tens of thousands of dollars in bail money and legal fees in an effort to extricate themselves. In the meantime, the Bank of Wisconsin had finally made good on a longstanding threat to foreclose on Taliesin, barring Wright from the premises in September 1926.

Within two years, many of Wright's possessions, including the bulk of his Japanese print collection, were sold at auction in satisfaction of his $25,000 mortgage. Digging himself out from the assorted claims of ex-wives, ex-husbands, banks, and other creditors would take Wright years. And, though he eventually succeeded, the consequences for his architecture were sharply negative: between 1925 and 1932 he completed only five buildings. Wright's lost years staggered into their second decade.

From "Prairie" to organic architecture

In the midst of all this tumult, Wright still found time to linger on some of the questions that had long preoccupied him as an architect. He had begun to write his autobiography, dictating it to a stenographer and finishing the first portion of it even while being pursued by the police. In it—as in other writings from around the same time—he began to elaborate what precisely he meant by organic architecture, and what the implications of it might be. "It is in the nature of any organic building," he wrote, "to grow from its site, come out of the ground into the light— the ground itself held always as a component basic part of the building itself." This kind of earthy, biomorphic rhetoric isn't too far from the principles Wright had been enunciating at least as far back as in the essay "The Art and Craft of the Machine." But the difference in context imparts a radically new meaning. Against the rising tide of what had been dubbed, by the late 1920s, the International Style of stringently simplified Modernism, Wright was striking a blow for the expressive and the idiosyncratic as opposed to the mechanized and the functional. And, with all his newfound notoriety, it was clearer now than ever before what kind of social order Wright had in mind when he spoke of fashioning a more "natural" social order: he was calling for a world in which individual action and expression are given the greatest possible scope, one in which the very purpose of society is to allow for the greater realization of the self.

"There has rarely been a moment during (Wright's) long career when he has not found an appreciative client among a group of open-minded, sincere American business men and women who realized from their own experience the value, or at least part of it, of what he had to give them ..."

Edgar Kaufmann

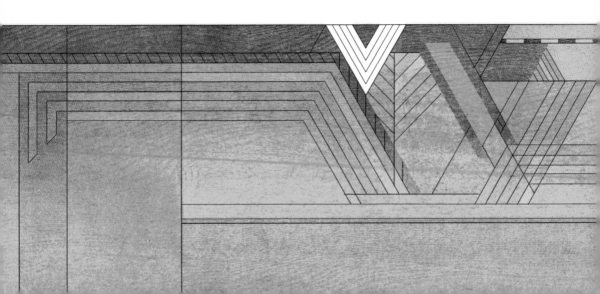

A new client

Miraculously perhaps—after all the bad publicity surrounding his personal life, all the disaffected clients, and the new class of Modernist architecture coming out of Europe—at least one client emerged in the 1930s who was not only prepared to take a risk on Wright, but who also appeared to truly understand and be receptive to his ideas. His name was Edgar J. Kaufmann, and the patronage of this Pittsburgh department store magnate was to alter the course of Wright's career.

For years, his son Edgar Jr.—who went on to become a respected professor of architectural history at Columbia University—claimed that it was he who arranged the first meeting between Wright and his father. In truth, it appears to have been Edgar Sr., known as E.J., who discovered Wright's work for himself, sought him out, and helped arrange an apprenticeship at Taliesin for his son in 1934. E.J. was invariably described as impetuous, energetic, and discerning—qualities that (along with a well-founded reputation as a philanderer) gave him much in common with Wright. The Kaufmann family came to Taliesin that year to meet Wright in person and, shortly thereafter, the architect had two commissions in hand, first to create a new private office for E.J. and then to design a house for the Kaufmanns on a site near their longtime summer retreat at Bear Run in southern Pennsylvania.

Edgar Jonas Kaufmann, Sr. pictured in his office at Kaufmann's department store in Pittsburgh.

Broadacre City

Among the first initiatives that can be credited to Kaufmann's involvement was the construction of a 12 by 12 foot (3.7 by 3.7 meter) scale model of an ideal American community of the future that Wright named Broadacre City. Built and exhibited in New York and Pittsburgh thanks to Kaufmann's largesse, this was organic architecture writ large, a world remade in Wright's own image: it was not a city in the conventional sense, but a semi-suburban cityscape–landscape where living, working, and playing would take place in a tranquil, natural setting that bore more than a passing resemblance to the Lloyd Joneses' beloved Valley. Reflecting Wright's contrarian, outsider status, the decentralized pattern and small-scale structures of Broadacre were a rebuke both to the hypertrophied metropolis of American capitalism and to the most provocative critique of the American city to date—Le Corbusier's proposed *Ville Radieuse*, the original "towers in the park" scheme of super high-rises surrounded by symmetrical lawns.

Every Broadacre family was to be allotted a one-acre plot for small, detached single-family units, while apartment buildings would be limited in number. Shared cultural and commercial facilities such as churches, arenas, restaurants, and community centers—all the prerequisites for communal life—would be in small clusters to be accessed by automobile via the extensive public roads. Highways were envisioned as straight ribbons of road with overpass–underpass concourses, while later iterations would imagine personalized helicopters floating like seed pods through the air. Wright's vision was of a society at once bracingly egalitarian and highly individualistic, with an entirely self-sufficient, autonomous economy.

Broadacre City scale model
Frank Lloyd Wright, 1935
Unbuilt

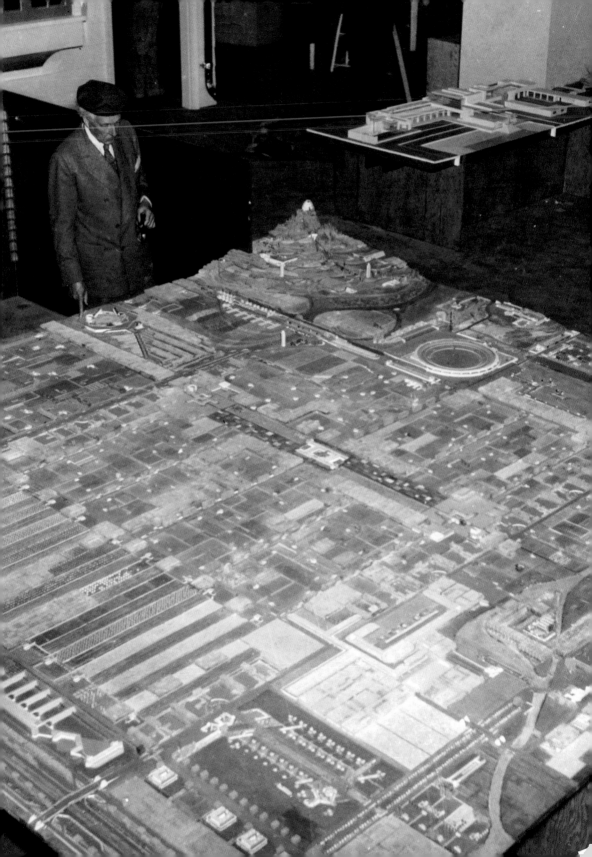

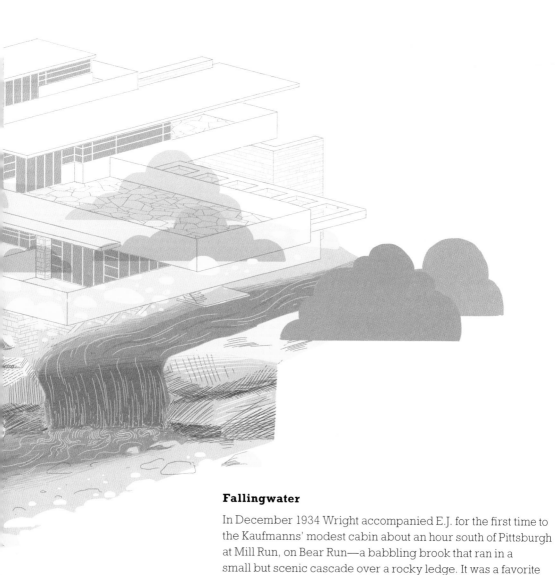

Fallingwater

In December 1934 Wright accompanied E.J. for the first time to the Kaufmanns' modest cabin about an hour south of Pittsburgh at Mill Run, on Bear Run—a babbling brook that ran in a small but scenic cascade over a rocky ledge. It was a favorite with the family as a bathing and picnicking spot. Wright was immediately taken with the site.

In their correspondence over the following months, Wright convinced Kaufmann to move forward with a new, and much grander, weekend retreat, and the contractual arrangements were set. Yet the promised plans did not emerge. Finally, exasperated, E.J. made a surprise visit to Taliesin. According to Wright folklore, the initial drawings were prepared in the few hours between Kaufmann's call and his arrival. What he saw amazed him: "I thought you would place the house near the waterfall—not over it!"

"The visit to the waterfall in the woods stays with me and a domicile has taken vague shape in my mind, to the music of the stream. When contours come, you will see it."

Frank Lloyd Wright

The design of Fallingwater was as daring, or more so, than anything Wright had attempted before: a structure dangling precariously over the rock face, its cantilevered decks making it appear a part of both the stream and the ledge itself. Kaufmann wasn't the only one amazed by the proposal and, in the ensuing two years of construction of the main house, the building contractor's objections to Wright's plans nearly prompted the architect to walk out. But when it came down to the wire, Kaufmann sided with Wright, and the house was built just as Wright intended.

Compositionally, the house comprises a series of intersecting perpendicular planes rendered in concrete, locally quarried river stone, and glass windows with red steel mullions. The chimney, as in so many of Wright's residential projects, is strongly expressed and central to the structure, but here the cantilevered domestic volumes almost seem disengaged from it, flying out over the waterfall.

Inside, the space is snug but warm, replete with Wright-designed furniture and surrounded on all sides by picturesque views of forest and stream. The furniture is all Wright's, and an ingenious trapdoor allows immediate access to the waterfall below. The Kaufmann family wasn't losing their favorite bathing spot: they would be able to go swimming any time they liked, straight from their living room.

The Kaufmanns' contractor may, in the end, have had the last laugh: the building has suffered from every type of leak, insulation failure, and structural slippage since the day it was completed, and has undergone extensive repairs several times since it opened to the public under the auspices of the Western Pennsylvania Conservancy in 1964. In the foregoing twenty years, while it remained in the Kaufmann family's possession, its staggering maintenance costs prompted E.J. to nickname it "Rising Mildew"—a term of endearment for a house that became, for all its problems, a beloved mainstay in the Kaufmanns' troubled family life.

Fallingwater
Frank Lloyd Wright,
1936–1939
Mill Run, Pennsylvania

"Truth Against the World"

With Fallingwater, Wright had delivered the object lesson he had been groping toward for nearly a decade: he had demonstrated the full architectural potential of organic design, producing a building so definitively modern yet so warm and earthy (and deliberately photogenic) that it caught the imagination of the public at once. In his autobiography, he had insisted that "'the machine for living in' is sterile," and now he had given architecture a compelling alternative. His stubborn contrarianism was paying off at last, bearing out the old Lloyd Jones family motto: "Truth Against the World."

Renaissance

The message came at the right time. The Depression was winding down, World War II was in the offing, and, by its end, the American people were looking for a new model for living in the twentieth century. They had the means to buy it, too, and increasingly they turned to Frank Lloyd Wright—written off only ten years earlier as a scandal-wracked fossil—to deliver it for them. Wright's lost years were over.

Johnson Wax Headquarters

Just two years after the completion of Fallingwater, Wright finished work on a project that showed what organic architecture could do for the work environment. The Johnson Wax Headquarters in Racine, Wisconsin, was Wright's most important corporate project since the Larkin Building, and it proved that the robust, original modernism of the Kaufmann house was no fluke.

The original low-rise building exuded a sleeker and more aerodynamic sense of monumentality than Larkin or any of Wright's older buildings, though it used the same long bands of brick and raked mortar that gave Robie its strong horizontal orientation. The 1939 structure was joined, in 1950, by a similarly soft-edged Research Tower.

But the design's most striking feature was what Wright termed its "lily pads," the tree-like interior columns that mushroomed from a diameter of just 9 inches (23 centimeters) at the base to 18 feet (5.5 meters) at the top. As at Fallingwater, the builders—and local regulators—expressed reservations about the system's viability, and insisted on stress testing to prove that they could withstand a load of 12 tons (10.9 tonnes). The columns did better than that: nearly 60 tons (54.5 tonnes) was placed atop them before they cracked.

Johnson Wax Headquarters
Frank Lloyd Wright, 1939
Racine, Wisconsin

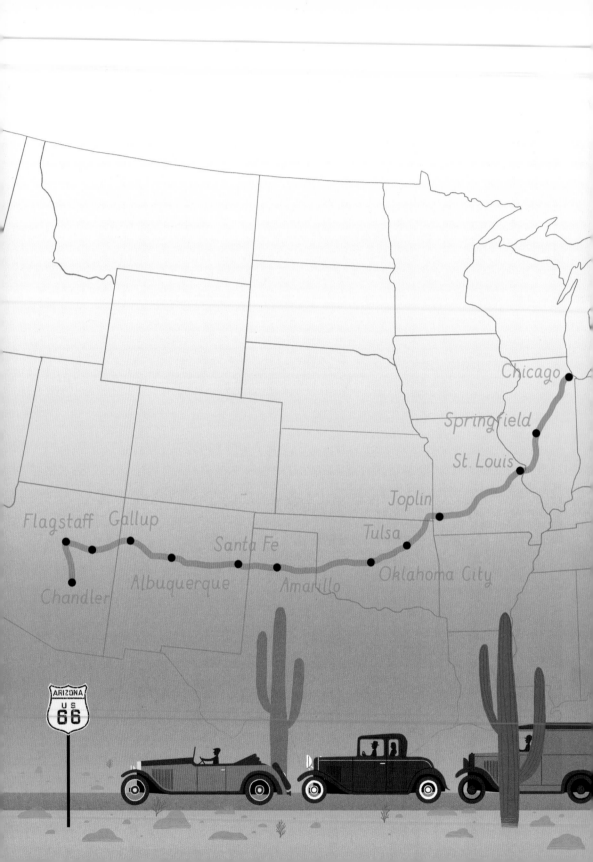

Taliesin West

Every year, from 1937 onward, Wright's students, associates, and assorted friends and family would make the long road trip from Wisconsin out to his winter home, Taliesin West, in Scottsdale, Arizona. The annual pilgrimage was one of many rites and rituals observed among the "Taliesin Fellows." Those enrolled in Wright's not-quite school were often obliged to perform menial tasks around the compound, from mixing cement to preparing food for Wright and Olga.

Wright had visited Arizona at least as early as the late 1920s, when he had come to Phoenix to consult on the construction of the Biltmore Hotel there. (The final design, though commonly misattributed to him, was not executed by Wright.) Drawn to the warm, arid climate and stunning desert landscape, he purchased property in nearby Scottsdale in 1937, and, within the year, had completed the first version of what was to be an ever-changing, ever-growing winter compound for himself and his group of young apprentices, the Taliesin Fellows. The Fellowship—part architecture school, part religious academy, part unpaid labor force—had been constituted in 1932 at Olga's prompting, and it reflected her, sometimes bizarre, spiritualist philosophy in addition to Wright's own imperious personality. But at Taliesin West, with on-site theater, music pavilion, and swimming pool, and with the barren beauty of the McDowell Range and Paradise Valley stretching out around them, the Wright circle formed a busy, if unorthodox, creative colony.

Taliesin West

Taliesin Fellow John Lautner working outside Taliesin West in 1940.

Fellows and family

Wright and Olga lorded over their Fellowship as if it were their personal fantasy realm. But it was one with more than its share of palace plots. Among the more improbable intrigues: when Olga's daughter by her first marriage, Svetlana Hinzenberg, died in a car accident, the bereft husband, William Wesley Peters—one of Wright's favorite apprentices—was later mysteriously maneuvered by his former mother-in-law into a new marriage with Svetlana Alliluyeva, Joseph Stalin's only daughter. As for Olga's only child by Wright, Iovanna Lloyd Wright was at once the community's untouchable princess and the subject of intense romantic interest among the young trainees. The combination made for a hothouse environment whose psychological effects would dog Iovanna for the rest of her troubled life. She died on September 7, 2015, in a nursing home in San Gabriel, California—the last link to a vanished creative kingdom that helped produce some of Wright's most outstanding work.

Unbuilt Wright

The rush of new commissions, and of eager young men keen to join the Taliesin Fellows, didn't mean that every one of Wright's proposals became a reality. In 1941, he proposed a series of low-cost Cooperative Homesteads for Detroit, Michigan, to be made using an innovative rammed-earth construction system. The war intervened, and the housing never took shape. In the 1950s, he was invited to Iraq by the wealthy Hashemite monarchy to devise a masterplan for the capital city of Baghdad; his designs included an elaborate opera house to be located on an island in the river Tigris, but all his ideas were swept away when King Faisal II's regime fell. While proposals like these came to nothing, others found their way into built form at a later date: in 1925, Wright developed a design for a combined museum–planetarium and "automotive objective" for Sugarloaf Mountain, Maryland. The structure was never built, but its inverted ziggurat-like form re-emerged 30 years later in one of Wright's final and most consequential projects—the unmistakable Guggenheim Museum in New York.

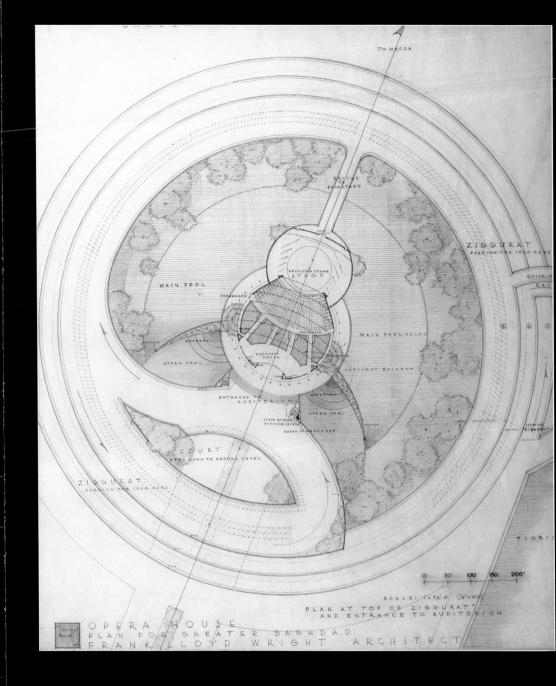

Plan for Greater Baghdad
Frank Lloyd Wright, 1957–1958
Unbuilt

Usonia

Wright's ambition to apply his organic principles on the largest possible scale was not confined to the grandiose "model train-set" version of Broadacre. As residential work began flooding back into the office, Wright adapted the Prairie house typology to a more thoroughly mechanized, more efficient World War II-era economy. The result was the Usonian houses: modest, single-family residences in a toned-down Wrightian style, complete with the signature built-ins, indirect lighting, custom-made furniture, and semi-enclosed breezeways. Sixty such houses were completed in Wright's lifetime, the closest Wright came to making his Broadacre dream a mass-market reality; it was a dream that anticipated, and in some ways helped to feed, the postwar suburban boom in America, as Wright's approachable Modernism became an aspirational commodity disseminated via glossy magazine covers and Hollywood films. (Watch Cary Grant clamber around a suspiciously Fallingwater-esque cantilever in *North by Northwest*.) Of course, few of the tract homes of the 1950s would have anything like the elegance of Wright's Usonia.

"Usonia" was a neologism that had been in circulation for some years prior to Wright's appropriation of it. It was meant as a synonym for "American," albeit with a snappier, more modern ring to it.

The "Usonian Automatics" were a subset of Usonian houses that deployed the concrete-block approach Wright had first pioneered in his early Californian projects. Wright hoped that the building system would allow would-be Usonian dwellers to construct their own homes. Few attempted it.

Applying the word to the houses gestured at their functional-yet-humanistic character. Usonian houses were perhaps not "machines for living in," as Le Corbusier espoused, but they were more aggressively minimalistic than Wright's earlier houses, featuring little or no ornament, far less expensive materials, and a focus on such convenient armatures as the "carport," Wright's signature automobile shelter.

In-floor radiant heating, gridded floor plans for easy construction, and less formal living spaces made Usonian houses both more economical and better adapted to the new, more casual style of family life. The ubiquitous American ranch house would later incorporate many of these elements.

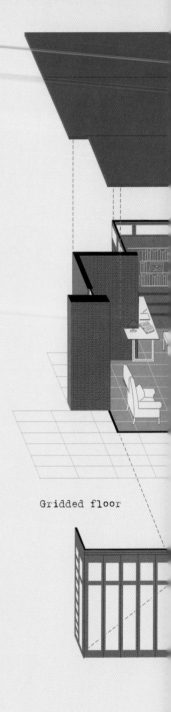

Gridded floor

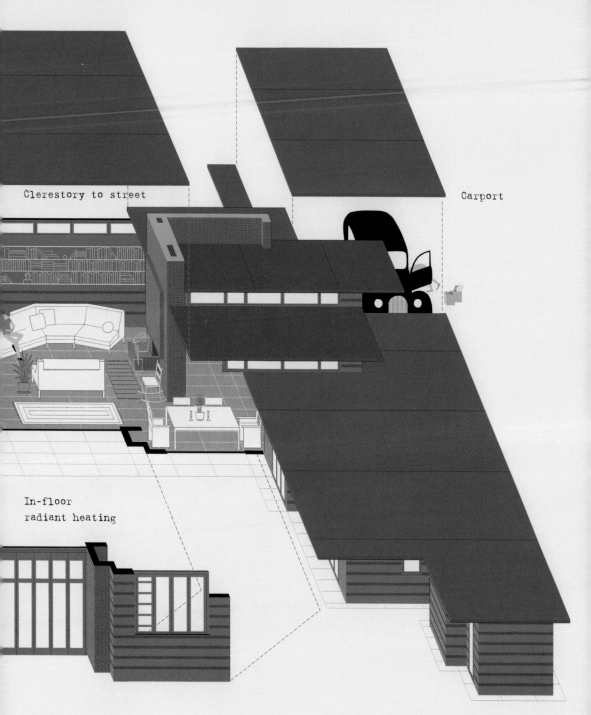

Clerestory to street

Carport

In-floor
radiant heating

Floor-to-ceiling
windows to the garden

Frank and Olga

Olga Lazovich Wright was a woman of rather eccentric, and very intense, enthusiasms. She believed that she and Wright were destined to forge a new world, and that whatever privations the Fellows were subjected to was worthwhile in the long run; she believed, too, that whatever extremes of emotional distress she might put Wright to were worth it as well, and the common coin of their relationship comprised infidelities, barbed exchanges, and passionate reunions. Whatever else it might have been, it was, in its own, odd way, functional: after two failed marriages, including an abandoned wife, and a number of minor affairs, Wright found in Olga his life partner.

The grand old man

He found something else, too. With the passing of time, Wright's various scandals acquired a certain sepia hue; divorce had become much more common after the war, and few begrudged Wright the family abandonment for which even his children (or most of them, anyway) had forgiven him. Wright had become something else: he had become an institution, a slightly absurd, but mostly lovable, national treasure. He opposed American involvement in World War II, his proclaimed pacifism somewhat tainted with an unseemly and anti-Semitic isolationism—but few seemed to mind, writing it off as just another instance of Wright being Wright. Some of his Fellowship graduates walked away exhausted, disillusioned, and angry—but many more had the time of their lives, even those who eventually fell out of love with the beloved Master and his witchy consort. Mies van der Rohe and Walter Gropius emigrated to the US, and with them they brought the International Style that became the urban vernacular for office towers and institutional buildings all across America—in particular, in Wright's adopted hometown of Chicago, where Mies became the reigning deity of the architecture scene in the same line of succession as Sullivan, "Uncle Dan" Burnham, and Wright himself. Yet, for the average American home-dweller, it was fusty, hoary old Frank Lloyd Wright who remained the sentimental favorite; and it was with his ideas that millions lived, in a sense, tucked inside their ranch houses on evenly parceled lots, surrounded by flagstones and fieldstones.

Wright's fluttering silk neckties harked back to the late nineteenth century Aesthetic Movement.

Porkpie hats and berets were favorites. As recently as the late 1990s, one of them fetched $6,000 at a Christie's auction.

At least one observer has traced a parallel to Oscar Wilde in Wright's cape fixation.

When walking around a site or building, Wright would jab his cane at the ground as he spoke in order to make his point.

Wright's style

Wright was known for his distinct sartorial style, what his son John referred to as "his picturesque free-and-easy clothes." It was a part of himself, and an extension of his practice: he took great care in selecting his own and his family's clothes. Instantly recognizable, the Wright "look" made the man as iconic as his buildings. The photographer Pedro Guerrero once said he was "a casting director's dream of what an architect should look like."

The Solomon R. Guggenheim Museum

His objective, Wright said, "was to make the building and the painting an uninterrupted, beautiful symphony such as never existed in the World of Art before." For this, one of his last and certainly most consequential projects, Wright returned in a sense to the typology of his earliest projects for the Lloyd Jones family: he would create a church, not to God this time but to art, and to the natural world that Wright believed was the wellspring of artistic inspiration.

Wealthy businessman Solomon R. Guggenheim, at the urging of his longtime art advisor and paramour Baroness Hilla von Rebay, had amassed a treasure trove of what Rebay termed "non objective" art, in particular abstract paintings by Paul Klee, Wassily Kandinsky, and others. Looking for a permanent repository for the collection, they turned to Wright, tasking him with producing a building that was not just a museum but a "museum–temple."

Wright did not disappoint. The interior ramps, modeled on a nautilus shell, wind around a central atrium topped by a glass skylight that floods the rotunda with natural sunlight. Wright's intention was that visitors would drift down the ramps, beginning at the top, though in practice most of the museum's shows have tended to be organized from the bottom up.

Despite its problematic organization, despite the inconvenience of looking at art on sloping walls, and despite the fact that its intended site, inside Central Park itself, had to be given up for the one across Fifth Avenue, the museum remains one of the most uncanny architectural environments in the US; it is an airy, sun-filled inverted ziggurat in the middle of skyscraper-shadowed Manhattan, a museum that feels as much like a poetic meditation on space and form as a place in which to look at art.

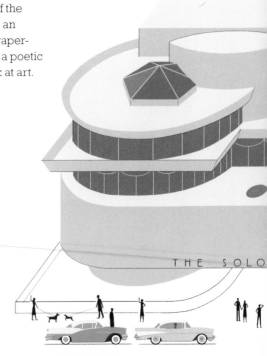

THE SOLO

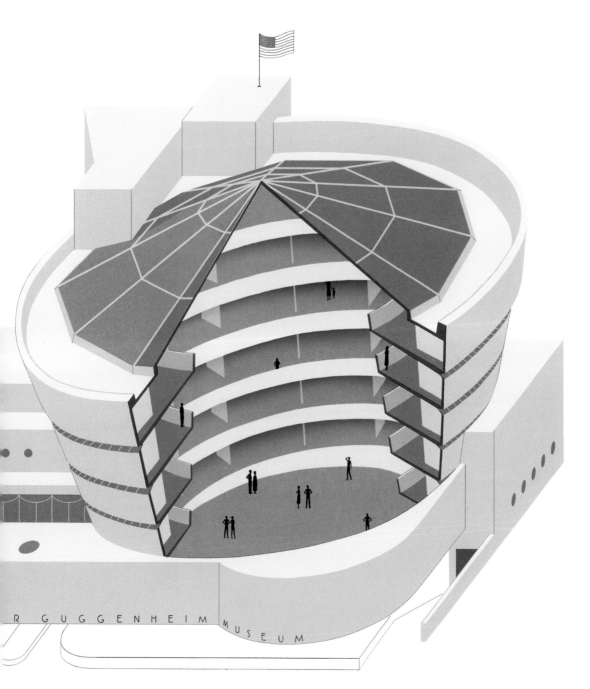

R GUGGENHEIM MUSEUM

"Death or no death, I see our countryside as a promise never to be broken."

Wright's final projects saw the architect still evolving, still changing in response to changing tastes and a changing world. The Price Tower (1956) in Bartlesville, Oklahoma was one of his only attempts (along with the Research Tower for Johnson Wax) at skyscraper construction; it reflected several bold and unrealized speculative proposals of Wright's, including one for a mile-high apartment building that he saw as a potential means to free up land for his Broadacre dream. In Dallas, Texas, the Kalita Humphreys Theater (1959) demonstrated a more restrained, austere approach than Wright had brought to his past public buildings and seems, in retrospect, almost to augur the coming wave of concrete-block Brutalist architecture that would sweep the American city a decade later. With all Wright's restless creative energy still very much in evidence at age 91, his Taliesin Fellows were taken somewhat unawares on April 4, 1959 when he came down with what seemed to be a stomach flu. He was admitted to hospital, but died on April 9. Two of the Fellows drove his body for 28 straight hours from St Joseph's Hospital in Scottsdale to Unity Chapel in Wisconsin, where he was buried in what was to have been a temporary grave pending the completion of a memorial chapel of his own design.

Legacy

The chapel was never built, and Wright's children and his last wife would carry on an ugly dispute for years as to where he had intended to be buried. The feud ended with the death of Olga: she had continued to operate the Fellowship through the early 1980s and, in her will, commanded that Wright be removed from Wisconsin to be buried next to her in Arizona. But the assorted entanglements of Wright's estate, his uncompleted work, and the continuation of his practice fairly pale next to the impact his ideas were to have on the design world: as the decades pass and tastes change, Wright's work has remained a touchstone for architects in the US and all over the world.

The Solomon R. Guggenheim Museum
Frank Lloyd Wright, 1956–1959
New York City

This was Frank Lloyd Wright

Wright's influence on subsequent generations of American architects has been profound. His pupil Rudolph Schindler, marrying Wright's attention to detail with a more restrained European approach, helped create a new style, the glamorous mid-century Modernism of Southern California; another Taliesin graduate, John Lautner, would take that style still further, creating some of the most iconic houses of the twentieth century. Bruce Goff, a longtime friend of Wright's, built houses that pushed Wright's sense of the natural world to its wildest, most eccentric limits, founding, almost by accident, the environmental movement in architecture. And decades later, when popular opinion had come around to Wright's view of the International Style as being barren and antiseptic, another Frank would emerge—working for the same client as Wright did in 1959— with a vision as original and as authentically American as Wright's: the architect was Frank Gehry, and the project was the Guggenheim Bilbao, one of the most important buildings of the last two decades.

"The mother art is architecture. Without an architecture of our own we have no soul of our own civilization."

Frank Lloyd Wright

And yet, for all his influence, Wright today is hardly at the center of architectural discourse. None of his particular stylistic qualities have ever been revived—none except his most slavish students ever wanted to "do" Frank Lloyd Wright after he was gone. His fear of the city and the skyscraper, and the mass suburbanism he advocated in Broadacre and elsewhere, have been roundly rejected by today's architects, who see urban density as key to sustainable design and to a truly ecological practice. And no architect now would dare set him or herself up as an all-seeing artistic demiurge, proving "Truth Against the World"! Wright's position in contemporary architecture seems just another one of the irresolvable contradictions of his life and character that have stymied critics and biographers for decades: he was a devout spiritualist and a venal materialist; a true innovator, and an unapologetic copier; a designer who always claimed to be expounding universal truths, but who also had a keen eye on his competition and a remarkable capacity to adapt. Perhaps the best and only understanding we can have of Frank Lloyd Wright comes not through his own professed ideas, nor through those of his various detractors and supporters, but simply through his buildings: monumentally non-monumental, and always indelibly human—in scale, in fallibility, in possibility.